FOREST BOOKS

THE ROAD TO FREEDOM

GEO MILEV was born in Radnevo, Bulgaria on 15 January 1895 and died at the age of 30 in 1925. He went to Sofia University when he was sixteen, but the following year continued his literary studies at Leipzig. During his short life he became known as a talented poet and artist. He also translated more than 50 books of prose, poetry and drama, enriching Bulgarian culture with his translations of writers such as Sophocles, Shakespeare, Omar Khayiam, Byron, Rilke, Verlaine, Verhaern, Pushkin, Blok and Mayakovski. He lost an eye in the First World War, but returned to Bulgaria determined to bring about a revolution of national cultural standards in all the arts. His ambitions were stifled when his new magazine *Plamak* (Flame), which was directed against the official terror at that time, was suppressed and he was arrested and brought to trial. After disappearing without trace his skull was found thirty years later in a pit near Sofia together with the bones of hundreds of other victims.

EWALD OSERS is a native of Prague but has lived in England since 1938. Among his published works are translations of over 90 books (24 of them poetry). He is also a poet and a volume of his own poetry has been translated into Czech and was published in Prague in 1986. He has also lectured on translation internationally. His awards include the Schlegel-Tieck Prize 1971, the C.B. Nathhorst Prize 1977, the Josef Dobrovský Medal 1980, the Goldene Ehrennadel des BdÜ 1982, the Silver Pegasus of the Bulgarian Writers' Union 1983, the Gold Medal of the Czechoslovak Society for International Relations 1986, the Dilia Medal, Czechoslovakia 1986, the Order of SS. Cyril and Methodius, Bulgaria 1986, the European Poetry Translation Prize 1987 and the Pierre-François Caillé Medal in recognition of his service to the translating profession.

D1603718

THE ROAD
TO
FREEDOM

Geo Milev

THE ROAD
TO
FREEDOM

Poems and Prose Poems
by
GEO MILEV

Translated from the Bulgarian
by
Ewald Osers

Preface
by
Leda Mileva

Introduction
by
Toncho Zhechev

FOREST BOOKS/UNESCO
LONDON ☆ 1988 ☆ BOSTON

UNESCO Collection of Representative Works
European Series
This book has been accepted in the translations
collection of the United Nations Educational Scientific
and Cultural Organisation (UNESCO)

PUBLISHED BY
FOREST BOOKS
20 Forest View, Chingford, London E4 7AY, U.K.
PO Box 438, Wayland, M.A. 01788, U.S.A.

First published 1988

Typeset in Great Britain by Cover to Cover, Cambridge
Printed in Great Britain by A. Wheaton & Co. Ltd, Exeter

Translations & drawings © Jusautor, Sofia
Photographs © Leda Mileva
Cover design © Ann Evans

British Library Cataloguing in Publication Data:
Milev, Geo
The road to freedom: poems
1. Title   II. Osers, Ewald
891.8'.113   PG1195.M5/

ISBN 0–948259–40–X

Library of Congress Catalogue Card No. 87–82775

Contents

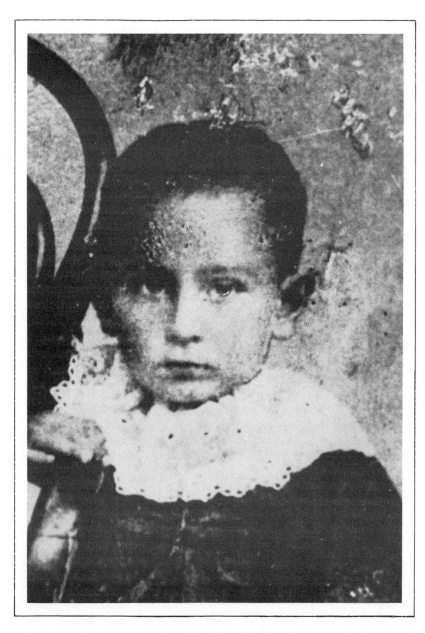

Geo Milev, 1897
(at the age of 2)

Introduction

Geo Milev is one of the most prominent figures in the development of Bulgarian literature — a banner of anti-fascist poetry, a volcanic temperament, an untamable spirit.

He was born on 15 January, 1895, in Radnevo, a village near the town of Stara Zagora, into a family of school-teachers. As a child, Geo Milev was a voracious reader, with a marked talent for drawing. His unusually intense development brought rapid and early maturity. While still very young he began to write poems, he edited hand-written newspapers and staged plays.

The precocious child started school at the age of five and became a university student in Sofia at sixteen. A year later, pursuing his literary studies, he was already in Leipzig. It was at that time he began his career as translator. During his short life-time of only 30 years, along with numerous other activities, he translated more than 50 books of prose, poetry and drama. Being a polyglot and a subtle interpreter, with a keen sense for the aristocratic, Geo Milev enriched Bulgarian culture with his translations of tragedies by Sophocles and Shakespeare, poems by Omar Khayiam, Byron, Rilke, Verlaine, Verhaern, Pushkin, Blok and Mayakovski, to mention only some of the authors he translated.

During the First World War he was called to the ranks as an interpreter. In April 1917, gravely wounded by an enemy shell, he lost an eye and part of his skull. He was sent to Germany for medical treatment and there underwent a series of surgical operations. But his restless and resourceful mind had a lot to offer to the war-weary world; it was full of bright ideas and radical projects for the rejuvenation of the old culture.

In a matter of days, to the utter astonishment of his doctors and nurses, he transformed his hospital room into an intellectual workshop piled high with books, papers and drawings. Impatient to establish new literary and artistic contacts, one day he decided he needed no more operations to 'restore his beauty'. The familiar portrait with a lock of hair, falling over the missing eye dates from that period.

In Berlin Geo Milev found himself the vortex of turbulent post-war Europe, at the centre of fashionable German expressionism, characterised by its quest for a radical reassessment of all values and for a new and vivid expressiveness. Geo Milev's contributions to *Die Aktion*, the periodical of the left-wing expressionists, were highly valued.

He returned to Bulgaria in 1919, filled with the spirit of rebellion and with a will to bring about a complete revaluation of national cultural standards. He founded and edited the magazine *Vezni* (Scales), which soon became the platform of Bulgarian modernism. A young man prone to extremes, Geo Milev launched a campaign for a 'new theatre', 'new literature', 'new music', 'new painting'. Some of the slogans raised in *Vezni* meant a total break-away from tradition and were doomed to remain an expression of vague longings. But the questions relating to Geo Milev's modernistic aberrations are extremely complex. Lately we increasingly tend to accept that they have played a major role in his attempt to find a language of his own, to acquire the unique revolutionary idiom for his immortal poem *September*.

In 1924, Geo Milev started a new magazine — *Plamak* (Flame). Although it existed for only a little over a year, it left a blazing trail in the history of the Bulgarian revolution press. To this day, as we turn the pages of the magazine, we get a burning sensation which is so fittingly symbolized by its title. It is significant that *Plamaka* began to appear right after the suppression of the 1923 September Uprising of the Bulgarian workers and peasants — the first anti-fascist uprising in the world. The magazine, as a whole, was directed against fascism, against the raging official terror and against those guilty of the large-scale massacres. Geo Milev's *September*, which appeared in the double issue (No. 7 and 8) of *Plamak*, belongs to the outstanding masterpieces of modern Bulgarian literature; it is an artistically impressive and powerful apotheosis of the mass-revolutionary struggle.

The issue which carried the poem was immediately seized by the authorities (suggesting that the police 'critics' had not failed to appreciate its significance). The author and editor of the poem were brought to trial. In the tragic days of April 1925, and during the massive repressions which followed a terrorist bomb explosion in the centre of Sofia, the poet disappeared without trace. It was not until the trial — 30 years later — of some of the organizers of the cold-blooded massacres of 1925 that shocking details came to light. The poet's skull, which he himself had described as a 'blood-stained lantern with shattered windows', was found in a pit near Sofia, together with the bones of hundreds of other victims.

'With the people, among the people' was Geo Milev's legacy. it was there, among the struggling people, that the tempestuous life of this great Bulgarian poet came to an abrupt end, to be born again in immortality.

Prof. Toncho Zhechev

Geo Milev with wife and two daughters, 1924

Footsteps on the Stairs

I hardly remember my father. I was less than five when he 'vanished without trace' — that was the first official version of his death in 1925. But, having grown up admist his family and friends, amidst his extensive multilingual library — Geo Milev's only real possession — my picture of my vanished father has always been vivid and sharp. His presence in our home was almost tangible. And because a phrase like 'vanished without trace' does not mean much to a little girl, for a long time I did not cease to believe that one day he would return. We were living in rented accommodation, as a rule on the top floor of various, for their time, tall buildings. Whenever I heard footsteps behind me as I climbed the stairs I always stopped and with a pounding heart timidly turned to see whether these were not, at long last, the footsteps of my father.

It was my mother who most often talked to me about him. My grandparents, with whom I spent all my school holidays in Stara Zagora, also spoke a great deal about him. And now, whenever I try to say something about Geo Milev the man, I rely principally on their memories.

My grandmother, who had borne and raised six children, maintained that her first-born son Georgi, because of his concentration and wide range of interests, had from earliest childhood stood out from the others. At first, at the age of only three or four, he had shown an exceptional liking for drawing. His father, who had a bookshop, had to bring him home a pad, pencils, and a paint-box. But the young artist painted not only on his drawing pad but also on the walls and on the cupboard doors. He soon began to draw whole pictures, as well as little horses and dogs. At primary school he made successful sketches of his teachers and of everyone else who attracted his attention. A little later he showed a passion for drawing caricatures, many of which are preserved to this day.

At the age of five he already knew the alphabet and declared that he wanted to go to school. At that time children entered the first form at the age of seven, and it was impossible for such a young child to be admitted as a pupil. But little Geo was so insistent that his parents were compelled to do something. They found a schoolmistress they knew and asked her to allow the child to attend school for a few days, so he could see for himself that it would not interest him. The teacher agreed. But things did not work out the way his parents had expected. Geo soon became a good pupil and continued to attend to the end of the year. The following autumn he was admitted as a regular second form pupil.

His interest in drawing and the representative arts continued as he grew up. This is confirmed by some ten self-portraits of Geo Milev which have been preserved. Other interests also appeared very early on in his life – the theatre, music, and the study of foreign languages.

All this began in the small provincial town of Stara Zagora, where the modest house of the bookseller Milyo Kasabov, with its large courtyard full of flowers, is now the Geo Milev Musem. The old well is still there and flowers still bloom. But the first thing to attract the visitor's attention is an enormous oak tree, growing between the well and the entrance, raising its trunk high above the brick wall which surrounds the courtyard, spreading its massive branches into the quiet street and rustling its green leaves almost as far as the houses on the opposite side. That oak tree, a rarity in Stara Zagora, famous as a town of lime trees, has its own history, told to me by my uncle Boris, my father's younger brother.

On Sunday mornings grandfather Milyo often took his two sons for a walk in the park by the railway station. One day the boys found some acorns there. 'Out of this small acorn can grow the biggest and most beautiful tree,' grandfather explained, 'a very healthy tree that can live more than a thousand years.' The boys each put a few acorns in their pockets and decided to plant them in the courtyard of their house. And in fact two small seedlings did grow from them. The boys dug around them and watered them, but Boris's tree soon withered. The oak planted by the elder brother, however, the majestic tree spreading its branches out over the little street which is now called Geo Milev Street, is approximately ninety years old. According to my uncle it was planted in 1900 or 1901.

Maybe it was from these early childhood experiences that the oak tree entered into Geo Milev's awareness as a symbol of majesty and tenacity. It appears in his poem *September* in the following lines:

> Blindingly
> over the Balkan peaks,
> with their navels turned
> to the sky
> and the eternal sun,
>   lightning flashes
>   — Thunder
> crashed
> straight into the heart
> of the giant
> hundred-year-old
> oak.

That poem also repeatedly refers to the Balkan mountain range which traverses Bulgaria from west to east. There, in a picturesque village on its flank, called Maglizh, my grandfather's family often spent several weeks during the hottest part of the summer.

Geo, by then a grammar school pupil, loved those holidays. He was moved by the beauty of the mountains. He would spend hours sitting on the high and not easily accessible Black Rock beyond the village, deep in thought, listening to the song of the Balkan mountains. My grandmother told me that on one occasion, as she was talking to some women in the village square, she turned towards the Black Rock. 'Can you see it?', she asked, 'An eagle sits perched on the rock.' The other women now turned their heads. 'Some eagle! Can't you see?', one of the women exclaimed, 'That's your son Geo!' His mother froze with horror. But the young eagle returned after a while, boldly and joyfully. From afar one could hear him singing his favourite song: 'Ah, forests, Balkan forests . . .'

Childhood and student years in Sofia and Leipzig, a visit to London which left a deep impression on him (reflected in his unfinished long poem 'Hell') soon passed, and the young poet found himself face to face with a grim reality. One rainy day he was sent to the fighting line. 'Throughout the day there is waste land all round,' he wrote in his wartime diary. 'Only the terrible whistle of the shells continually reiterates the terrible thought: "War!".'

Soon he was to experience its full horror. In the spring of 1917 fierce enemy artillery fire cracked his skull. Geo lost his right eye. Only by a miracle did he survive. Yet in spite of his severe wounds he was still fired by a desire to read, to work with all his strength, to ensure that he lived a full and valuable life.

Against his parents' objections, and before he was fully recovered, he married a young actess and intellectual, Mila Keranova, who had recently returned from Paris where she had studied philology at the Sorbonne. And although they had little money, the young family was soon increased by two daughters.

Our home, which I remember vividly, was in the very centre of Sofia, by the market hall. Under the windows of the big building, which before the war had been the post office, the trams clanked by. With the acute shortage of accommodation after the war many families were crowded into that building. And so we lived in one large room on the fourth floor; that room contained everything – bedroom, children's nursery, study.

My mother has left an accurate account of the circumstances in which her husband worked, feverishly and untiringly for the next five years. 'He wrote on a small plain table [which is now in the Geo Milev Museum] in his small, modest but interesting study,' my mother recorded in her memoirs. 'One wall of his study was taken up by his large library, and the opposite wall was formed by a screen which divided off the bedroom. On the study side the screen was painted by Geo with cubist figures and in the middle it had a small door with a curtain of dark blue cloth to which I had stitched some golden stars and a crescent moon cut out by Geo. By the table Geo had a small settee with many cushions, painted by him and embroidered by me. I used to sit there and listen to Geo reading to me. He smoked a lot, and would get me to make him strong coffee. Geo was infinitely considerate towards me and the children.

Clearly there was not a lot of room for us children and we often played with our dolls under the table in the bedroom behind the screen. Friends of my father's would say that no matter what time of night they passed our building there was always a light in our window. 'Geo is working,' they said.

In spite of his unbelievable amount of work my father had many friends – mainly writers, artists and painters, who sometimes interrupted his evening's work on his manuscripts and noisily thronged our flat. 'Those meetings,' my mother recalled, 'were rapturously bohemian. We always had to scrape together everybody's meagre means in order to prepare a dinner. But they were meetings with rich literary programmes, not planned, of course, but as soon as Geo stood at the centre it was impossible not to recite verse or talk about the theatre, or sing songs in all the languages we knew. Geo was carried away, forgetting that the following morning they would call for the proofs. But these evenings in a circle of friends were his only relaxation.'

At that time the fascist government of Bulgaria proclaimed its ominous 'Defence of the Realm' law. My mother has often told me that as soon as she read the first few sections of the then unfinished poem 'September' she saw herself as a widow and her children as orphans. She did not conceal from her husband this terrible premonition. But he only laughed and tried to reassure her. 'This is a literary work; have no fear! Don't cry, it's useless, no one and nothing can stop me. I must finish and publish this poem.'

Even after the confiscation of No. 7/8 of the periodical *Plamak*, in which the finished poem was published, and despite several police searches of the house, my father had no intention of emigrating or even of leaving Sofia, although his friends were advising him to do so. One of my few clear memories from that time is the morning of our unexpected parting. I can still see the dark silhouette of the policeman framed in the door as he summoned my father for 'a little questioning'. My mother gave him a clean handkerchief and he followed the policeman out without even saying goodbye — surely they were just summoning him for a little questioning and he would soon be back for his morning cup of coffee.

I remember very clearly how, soon afterwards, my mother started searching for him from one precinct to another, from one prison to another, from one town to another. I used to go off to school, and when, returning home, I would hear footsteps behind me on the stairs I used to stop. My heart would pound. I would turn timidly. But my faint hope would again dissolve. No, these were not the footsteps of my father who had been summoned to the police station 'for a little questioning'.

Leda Mileva

Geo Milev, 1912

from the film
'On the Tracks of the Missing'
(based on the book of the same title by Nicholai Christosov)

EXPERT: Gentlemen, poetry as an art recognizes neither science nor party spirit. The poet sings for art's sake. He rides a throne high above the petty things in life. He doesn't take sides. He does not praise some in order to insult others. He only depicts everything he sees in tender and beautiful shades of poetry. And when the reader understands his writings, he sees there a colourful, non-photographic depiction of an episode of life. Unfortunately here we have a writing in contradiction to the above, which is a vulgar challenge to vice, enflaming animal instincts . . . and all this in a tormented country, which, most of all, needs peace. We have in fact a poem called 'September', which depicts the people in mean and insulting ways, giving untrue images of contemporary life. It should be burned out.

CHAIRMAN: Final judgement on criminal action no. 249 of May 14, 1925 at the Third Penal Session of Sofia county court. For writing and publishing the poem 'September' in *Plamak* magazine, on the authority of art. 7 of the Law for Protection of the State, the poet Geo Milev is sentenced to one year close confinement, a fine of 20,000 levs and deprivation of civil and political rights for two years . . . This sentence is final.

GEO MILEV: Mr Chairman, we cannot write that the people is happy when it is drenched in blood, we cannot sing of rosy aroma and birds, when we hear nothing but the cry of mothers in black . . . we are contemporaries of a great moment in history — the waking up of the people, its evolution from 'herd' into nation. The people think, in spite of the ardent desire of some or others not to . . .

PROSECUTOR: Mr Milev, speak only to the points of the indictment.

GEO MILEV: That's exactly what I'm doing, Mr Chairman. Today, I'll be sentenced for a poem. Why? Just because it is entitled 'September'. If this is a nightmare for guilty conscience

I am not to be blamed for that . . . *Plamak* may be banned, the poem 'September' may be destroyed with it, but there are no firemen in the world who can put out the flames of thought and even less of the idea of humaneness and peace forever, which is the idea of all poets. So far the world has never known a poet to be sentenced for poetry. The Bulgarian Court faces a great problem — can a poet be sentenced for his poem?

CHAIRMAN: Have you anything more to say, Mr Milev?

GEO MILEV: Yes, Mr Chairman. Poetry blossoms on the soil of freedom. Do not harass the writer or you'll kill art.

ROMANIA

BULGARIA

Varna

Black Sea

SOFIA

Nova Zagora

YUGOSLAVIA

TURKEY

GREECE

Acknowledgements

We wish to thank the Sofia Press for allowing us to reproduce the English translation of *The Road to Freedom & Other Poems*, edited by Tatyana Egert, translated by Ewald Osers, 1983; Jusautor for permission to reproduce the drawings from the Bulgarian edition of 'September', Sofia 1983; and Bulgarian radio and television for permission to reproduce excerpts from the play 'On the Tracks of the Missing'.

We would also like to thank Leda Mileva for her help and interest and for allowing us to reproduce family photographs; the Union of Translators and Writers of Bulgaria for their help and encouragement; and David Bailey for research and editorial assistance.

Cover photograph: self-portrait by Geo Milev

'It is too often forgotten that the Tzankoff Government, which came into power by the murder of its predecessors ... that has kept its power by terror under cover of a series of political assassinations, has a terrible history, and the best thing that could happen to Bulgaria would be that it should have a new Government which might come into power without assassination and terrorism, a new Government based on a new election.'

Colonel Wedgwood MP, House of Commons, 28 May 1925
(Hansard)

All roads lead to Rome. Only one leads to Paradise: the road of Freedom.

(Geo Milev: 'May')

September

1.

Born from the night's dead womb
is the age-old wrath of the slave:
Scarlet and awesome his ire —
like fire.

Deep amidst darkness and mists.

From dusky valleys
before the day dawns
from every mountain
from barren scrub
from hungry farmland
from hovels of mud
from village
and town
from farmyard
cottage and croft
factory, warehouse and railyard
from barn
and farm
mill and
workshop
power-plant
shopfloor:

by road and winding lane
high up
by scree and gorge, rocky peak and ridge
by field path
and hillside
along rocky cliffs
through autumn-yellow woods

over boulders
and water
and turbid ditch
through meadows
and gardens
cornfields
vineyards
shady sheepfolds
hawthorn
burnt stubble
brambles
marshes: ragged
muddy
hungry
sullen
haggard from toil
coarsened by heat and cold
misshapen
crippled
tangle-haired
barefoot
scarred
simple folk
savage
angry
frenzied
                — without roses
                and song
                without music or drums
                without clarinets, kettledrums, lanterns,
                french horns, trombones, trumps:
on their backs tattered packs
in their hands no gleaming swords
but simple sticks

Sofiotes with cudgels
with bars
with goads
with picks
with pitchforks
with hatchets
with axes
with scythes
and sunflowers
— old and young —
a flood-tide from everywhere
— like a blind herd
let loose
numberless
raging bulls —
shouting
howling
(behind them the night's stony vault)
forward they flew
in disorder
      irresistible
      terrible
      great:
      THE PEOPLE!

2.

Night scattered amidst the brilliance
on the peaks.
The sunflowers
gazed on the sun!

Dawn awoke
from sleep
to the rattle of machine-guns:
from distant
hillsides
— crack after crack —
came the lash
of mad
bullets and lead.
Cannon
like elephants' jaws
roared . . .
Trepidation and fear.
The sunflowers dropped in the dust.

3.

Vox populi:
                    Vox Dei.
Stabbed
by a thousand knives
the people —
dulled
degraded
lower than even a beggar,
left
without brain
without nerve —
rose up
from the troubled darkness
of its life
— and with its blood wrote:
                              FREE!

Chapter One:
               September.
— Vox populi —
— Vox Dei —
O God!
Support Thou the sacred work
of coarsened black hands:
pour Thou boldness
into our pounding hearts:
Thou wishest no man a slave —
behold — we swear by our grave —
we shall raise up man free
yes, free in the world.
Ahead of us is death —
                    So let it be!
But beyond:
Canaan blooms
promised to us
by Truth —
eternal spring of a living dream . . .
We believe! We know! We wish it thus!
God is with us!

4.

September, September!
O month of blood!
Of upsurge
and rout!
Maglizh was first

Stara
and   } Zagora
Nova
Chirpan
Lom
Ferdinand
Berkovitsa
Sarambey
Madkovets
            (with the priest Andrey)
— townships and villages.

5.

The nation rose up
— with a stick
in its hand,
covered in soot and in sparks and in cinders
— with a sickle amidst furrows,
damp and cold to the marrow:
the folk of black toil
with ineffable suffering —

                    (not geniuses
                    intellects
                    demonstrators
                    agitators
                    speechifiers
                    aviators
                    entrepreneurs
                    restaurateurs

                                        musicians
                                        morticians
                                        generals
                                        writers
                                        pedants
                                        and Black Guard fighters)

But
peasants
workers
unsophisticates
havenots
illiterates
simple and coarse
hooligans
and boars
— a rabble like beasts:
                              thousands
                                        masses
                                                 the people:

thousands of faiths
— faith in the people's rise
thousands of wills
— will to a happy life
thousands of turbulent hearts
— and fire in every heart
thousands of blackened hands
— in the wide red expanse
eagerly raising
red
banners
unfurled
            high
            wide

over the whole land rocked by unrest and alarm,
frenzied fruit of the storm:
                        Thousands —
                        masses —
                        the people.

6.

A flash
over the native Balkans,
with their navels turned
to the sky
and the eternal sun,
                        of lightning
                        — Thunder
crashed
straight into the heart
of the giant
hundred-year-old
oak.

Hill after hill
onward dispatched
the rapid echo
over ridges
and boulders
to steep-sided valleys
into rocky crannies
— those fiery beds,
where vipers and grass-snakes
sleep in coils,

into the caves
of dragon brood,
into the hollow tree-trunks of witches

        —and the thunder merged
        with the distant echo:
        thunder and roar
        of waterfalls
            torrents
            and streams —
            with thunder and hiss
            furiously hurtling
            down the abyss.

7.

The tragedy begins!

8.

The first
fell in blood.
The rebellious surge
was met by lead.
The flags dropped
riddled.
The mountain reverberated.

18

Up there
on hills far and near
appeared
men
— swelling
black ranks:
regular paid troops these —
and enraged police.
They all understand:
'The fatherland
is in danger!'
          Very fine:
          but — what is the fatherland?
And the machine-guns
are furiously barking . . .

The first
fell in blood.
Beyond distant hills
came the crash of artillery.
Towns
and villages
shook.
Dead bodies
— blood-drenched piles —
covered
hillsides
and roads . . .
With drawn swords
cavalry squadrons
pursued routed peasants
— shattered and shot
by shrapnel and mortar
— scattered in terror in all directions,

chased to their homesteads
and hacked down
with bloody swords
under low eaves
amidst the shrieks
of terrified mothers
and children and wives . . .

— — — — — — — — —

9.

The troops advanced.
Under the terrible crump of shrapnel
even the bravest
quailed:
in despair
bare hands were raised to heaven.
Horror without glory
froze on every face —
eyes without tears
            'Everyone
            save
            himself!'
By every road
company follows company
            — infantry
            cavalry
            artillery.
            Drums
            beat the charge.
            Panic
            — high and large

35

above the torn
scarlet banners
the crimson whip of fire is borne.

There,
as chaos progressed,
alone
like a man possessed,
bold
like a hero of old,
the priest Andrey
fired
shell after shell
from the famous gun . . .
At last,
yelling
'Death to Satan!'
with magnificent wrath
he turned
his cannon:
his final shot
he dispatched
straight
          — at the house of God,
where he'd sung litany and liturgy.
Then he surrendered.
'Hang him by a length of rope:
no cross or grave for the red pope!'

He was taken to a telegraph pole.
By it stood the hangman.
The captain.
The noose
was ready.

The Balkans
were shrouded in cloud.
The sky
was cruel.
The priest stood erect
to his full size,
all
calm as granite —
without lament
without remembrance
— Christ's cross on his breast
his gaze on the crests
far away
as though on the future . . .
— You fearfully lower your eye
at the moment a man died,
you butchers!
But what is the death
of one man?
Amen! —
He spat
at their feet.
Quickly he
himself slipped the noose
round his neck
and
without a glance at the sky
— he dangled —
tongue clenched in his teeth,
strangled:

great
sublime
unattainable!

10.

Autumn
flew by
in wild shreds
of wailing and gale and night.
Storm broke loose
over dark mountains

— blackness and flash
and the croaking of ravens —

A sweat of blood
broke from the earth's back.
Cottage and hut
cowered in fear.
Death rides here!
Thunder
rent the sky asunder.

11.

That was the start
of the worst horror.
Frenzied with fury
alarm bells rang out in each heart
— struck, pealed, rang —
Night fell on the land
with silence and terror confined
on all sides.

Death
— a blood-thirsty witch
lurking in every dark corner —
shrieked
as far and wide
with her dry bony fingers
— so long, oh so long —
she seized, tore apart
each terrified heart
behind every wall.
O night of nameless dark scenes!
— some hidden, some seen:

Village squares once more stained scarlet with blood.
The rattle of death from throats cruelly cut.
The ill-boding clanking of chains.
Jails crowded again.
From prison yards, barrack squares
comes the shout
of commands.
Volleys ring out.
Doors are locked.
Strange visitors hammer at them.
The son, with pistol cocked,
lies dead on the threshold.
Father hanged.
Sister defiled.
Peasants driven from villages
escorted by troops:
a dismal convoy
bounded for the firing squad:
A voice rings out: Halt!
'Fire' —

A clicking of bolts:
                    Ku
                        Klux
                            Klan —
'Fire'
        — bang.
Ten bodies
heavily tumbled
from the river bank
into the turbid dead waters of the Maritsa.
Discoloured with blood
the river in sorrow bears them on its flood.
An army band in a deserted street
booms out
'Maritsa, river sweet . . . '
River of blood . . .
In trampled fields
amidst thorns
among thistles and tall grasses
roll crimson heads
with mutilated faces.
Gallows stretch out their black arms
(spectres in deathly haze).
Ceaseless the terrible march of the axe
as it strikes against bone. Farmsteads ablaze
light up the horizon.
Torrents of blood still flow.
Pyres with fiery glow
with blasphemous tongue of flame
like the sacred frame
of God's
throne.
A small of flesh burning.
A horrified shout

rings out
from the blessed in paradise
— a savage Hosanna to God —

The end.
The hurricane has passed,
the storm
has stopped at last.
Peace
and quiet
have fallen
on the whole
land.
A bloody sacrifice to the gods.

12.

Sing, O Muse, of the fateful wrath of noble Achilles . . .

Achilles was brute force.
A military demon.
Achilles was the senior general
of H.I.M. King Agamemnon.
Achilles was a hero.
With countless
crosses and orders and ribbons . . .
The pillar
of peace and order
in the land . . .

But we today
no longer believe in heroes
— neither foreign, nor our own.

Troy was burnt down and sacked.
Priam and Hecuba perished.
Achilles triumphed . . .
— What's Hecuba to him? —
His soul is wild and grim
he does not hear
the crying of the holy mother, distraught
over nameless graves bedewed with blood
that have sprung up in a moment
— so many —
numberless.
— What's Hecuba to him? —
Achilles was a hero.
Achilles was great.

A divine scourge sent by God.

Yet Achilles will perish under wrath
                                    and curses!
And he perished
                he died a shameful death:
just venegeance on a killer.
Agamemnon killed Iphigenia
                — and perished:
Clytemnestra killed Agamemnon
                — and perished:
Orestes with Electra killed Clytemnestra
                — and perished:
Left alone
— standing and enduring

through centuries —
is Cassandra the prophetess:
she prophesied retribution
— and everything came to pass.
Constant diversion, game and entertainment
of the gods.
Eternal flowering of divine viciousness.
Every death, to them, is amusement,
all tears a joke.
Death, murder and blood!
How long, how long?
All-powerful Zeus
    Jove
    Akhuramazda
    Indra
    Toth
    Ra
    Jehovah
    Zeboath:
— answer me!

From smoke and flames rise
to your ears the cries,
the screams of the dead,
the howl
of numberless martrys
on stakes of burning wood.
— Who
betrayed our faith?

Answer me!
You're silent?
You don't know?

We do know!
Behold
with one leap, with one nod,
we jump straight into heaven:

— we hurl a bomb at your heart,
we'll take your heaven by storm:

and from your throne
we dispatch you dead
down to the depths of the universe,
unstarred
iron-hard —

By heavenly bridges
high beyond measure
with towers embrasured
we'll bring Paradise down
to earth,
this grief-overgrown
blood-overflown
earth of ours.

All that was written by poets, philosophers
shall come true that day!
— Without God! Without master!
September will be May.
Human life
will be one endless forward drive
— higher still! higher still!
Earth will be Paradise —
it will!

A Little
Expressionist
Calendar
for 1921

January

That day I was born.
That day, between icy teeth of the cold, the last howl of
the blizzard suddenly fell silent. The Great Bear bristled
frozen — all white — with ice; between its gleaming white teeth
the crumbled disk of the North Star.

The silence and motionlessness of the blue frost; under the
unquivering glow of the Northern Lights.

On the threshold of my destiny stands that white-haired old man
Aquarius; my destiny's unceasing stream that he is pouring out —
it has frozen up, my destiny.

That day I was born and my heart, newly born, instantly froze up:
a huge bright lump of ice.

I believed a translucent bright angel would carry my heart in his
gentle fingers — far from the blessed bourns. He did not come:
the gentle heart expired in the frost's icy nails.

That day I was born. My heart froze up: a huge lump of ice.

I do not love. My heart is ice, a stone, iron, cruel.
I love nothing, no one. I do not love!

O book of enmities!

I am clutching my heart in my hand — that huge lump of ice —
and I wait: ready for battle.

Woe to soft foreheads!

February

Thousands of factory chimneys constrict the azure circle of
the horizon. And black dragons — of sparks and soot — spread
huge shaggy wings over the grey suburbs.

Where is God's azure smile? The world is without a sky.
The world is without love . . .

Spite. Hostility. Beneath the black wings of the angry dragons
of sparks and soot. Merciless murder of the azure.

And in the evening, when thousands of sirens emit a horrible
whine far out to the black fields — O black hands of labour,
shaking with spite and hostility . . .

O angry song of those black hands!

Open up the azure circle of the horizon. Give us back the sky!

The sky! The sky! The sky!

March

Behold the first crimson morning.
Behold the crimson trumpets of the morning's glow.
The drumbeat of the melted drops.
The battlecry of the southern wind.
And the heavy cannonade of the bursting ice.
Behold the grey banners of hunger, dipped in prayer
amid the battlefields of spring.
A beginning!
Behold the sun's scarlet shield in our black hands.
We raise it boldly — forward — into battle.
The sun.
And at that moment: behold, the first thunder of spring.

April

Sages and poets breathe the pure air in springtime gardens
at nightfall, above their clear-ringing brows hangs the
deep mystery of the nocturnal sky — ultramarine and silver —
above the quiet arabesque of the intertwined young tendrils
of vines and the blossoming boughs of appletrees.

Innumerable question-marks in the nocturnal sky —
and the silvery alarm of Tycho Brahe.

Not long ago I found myself on its bank. Yet my hollow
hand caught nothing from the eternal river. In vain . . .

Is there a God?

Above the clear-ringing brows of the sages and poets
the sky yawns with bottomless silence — ultramarine and
question-marked.

Somehwere are the bright lights of noisy restaurants.
And through the shadow of the white springtime gardens —
at just that time in the late evening — passes, long-strided,
the gigantic silhouette of a black man.

May

Once there was spring, and summer, and all the rest of the seasons. Once there was May.

Once, with the first warm breath of the springtime seas, the swallows arrived in noisy arched flights and the love-lorn nightingales arrived — and red-blushing roses bloomed under every window.

Once . . .

Never!

There never was any spring, or May, or swallows, there were no love-lorn nightingales and no roses under every window. There never was an idyll, there was never Theocritus or Virgil.

Swallows and nightingales exist only in textbooks of zoology; and May is a torrent of heavenly water which ceaselessly, day and night, drenches the muddy roads in the darkness of dreadful damp night, when through the dim light of a lonely lamp in a deserted street the black silhouette of a man passes with firm steps, a man with a pack on his back and with a tearful child stumbling behind him.

Who hurries so late through rain and dark?

June

One madman, one King Lear, stands all alone amidst an empty square, under the stormy midnight sky which cracks flashes of lightning over the frightened town.

Lear declaims:
> O thunderbolts, O lightning from high heaven!
> Shake, crack o'er human vanity and sin!
> Heaven and earth and hell! Almighty God!
> O Satan! — and so forth.

— What are you doing here, friend? his buffoon asks him with a wooden smile.
— I'm singing a song of love and truth!

Amidst a moment of silence in the storm somewhere in the distance a homeless dog utters to the sky a prolonged and horrible howl of death.

July

The torried wilderness of the world suddenly freezes
in its fear: O the terrible roar of the lion; O the
terrible roar of hunger and righteous anger.

And London and Paris and New York are seeking shelter
in the caves of the night. O night and tombs with no prey
for the hyenas.

The world's wilderness freezes in its fear.

The hungry king of the wilderness utters a terrible roar
for paradise. Ready for a blood-thirsty leap for conquest
and revenge.

O terrible roar of hunger and righteous anger!

August

Your lair is behind the drawn dark-crimson curtains,
O beautiful beast! O luscious fully-ripe Virgo! tender
sacred nudity in the lampsade's rose-coloured half-light
in the clammy bedding of langour . . . In the heart of the
stifled memory of that first drop of blood, dissolved
in the pre-vernal snow . . .

You are one under all skies — far from the deadly wastes
of space, unruffled by the horror of time.

You are the one and only and eternal — and your name
is Mary.

Rejoice, immaculate Virgin! — before your langour steps the
angel of the spirit, adorned with the white lilies of
annunciation. He plants in your heart the heavenly stalk
from which shall spring the flower of Worldwide Happiness.

Rejoice, immaculate Virgin! — you will be the mother of the
freedom of the spirit, you will be the mother of human
                                                brotherhood,
you will be the mother of worldwide equality.

September

When at midnight on the seventh floor I open the
oppressive window high above the city — in the
infinity of the dusky horizons tremble countless
scattered lights — windows, shopfronts, streetlamps —
the city lies there like a huge thousand-headed, thousand-eyed
hydra which one day will suddenly rise up, terrible and
ferocious: before lighted windows with silken curtains,
over carefree roofs, beneath which chords ring out on
pianos, orchestras and gramophones, where fat thighs
recline in smoothly ironed trousers on soft plush sofas
and settees — over stages decorated with paper flowers
female legs are dancing, half-veiled by transparent little
tulle dresses, amidst champagne bared breasts are swaying
before rude glances roused by lust.

O ferocious hydra of retribution, thousand-headed,
thousand-eyed with the countless lights of the nocturnal
city awaiting the twelfth hour.

Far away, from the womb of the black clouds, a bloody
moon is born.

October

The wide boulevard shoots out into the infinity
of the suburbs.

The noisy boulevard dies in a single instant —
deserted — carried away into the hazy infinity
of the suburbs. Along the two sides of the distant
boulevard, walking slowly, one behind the other,
are black men with rifles. Abandoned trams and cars
stand frightened amidst the deserted boulevard, looking
out from large empty eyes. And rapidly heavy shutters
crash down in front of the doors of the big stores.
From upper floor windows the curious faces of sweet
servant girls peer shyly.

In the distance, from the hazy infinity of the wide boulevard
a huge wave of black people comes flowing — illuminated
by the golden glow of autumnal trees.

From somewhere comes the terrible chatter of teeth
of machine-guns.

Somewhere monocles and binoculars focus on colourful
jockeys racing; the galling curiosity: Bucephalus
or Adler? The heavens are bursting into tears. By
the entrance of the racecourse poor women and blind
men are selling matches, cigarettes, pencils and chestnuts.
Among them a blind man in a faded military tunic puts
down a straw hat with a frostbitten broken hand.

From somewhere comes the sound of gunfire.

The wide boulevard is lost in the hazy infinity of
the suburbs which are still dispatching their black
people. Autumn is gilding them.

November

When the great human wave gigantically and alarmingly
engulfs buildings, roofs, towers — O the crash and
crack of beams and tiles under its weight — and the
mighty roar of the last surge — and the despairing,
frightened scream. Rebellion!

We are building barricades: boxes, casks, bales of
paper: O jerking of wiry muscles — barricades with
red flags over them.

High above the roofs chatter the insolent machine-guns:
dizzy gyration — crowds, squadrons, cannon, armoured
cars — in the streets, squares, courtyards . . .

Suddenly in front of the Guards' barracks: two terrible
ranks of riflemen with red bands on their arms.

We are building barricades, we are digging a trench:
between Yesterday and Tomorrow.

Spartacus!

December

Through rain and snow and gloom and wind
and blood we are going towards the bright
manger of God.

Through the endless world — toil and suffering —
our star leads us along the white road of distant
winter. Faith leads us and our star.

Let a quiet gleam warm our black broken hands.
Let the opened heavens make blissful our hearts
with a song of golden strings and silver tintinnabulations
and the bright voices of heavenly angels: Hosanna!
Hosanna! Peace on earth — good will toward men!

The heavens open and we enter through their diamond
gates.

And with joy we bow our wrinkled black brows before
the bright manger of the new God.

Immaculate Virgin, from your heart springs a white
rose — O white wreath over the black cross of our
sufferings. We bow our black brows.

And the radiant child in your lap with a smile raises
a benedictory hand over us and says:

Peace unto you!

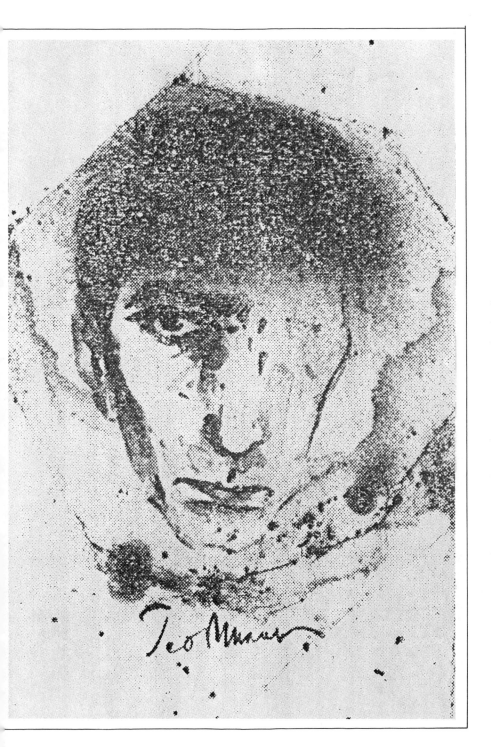

Self-portrait

Ugly Prose

Faith

O disillusioned, disenchanted, distressed, sinful, sorrowful,
helpless, wretched, corroded, agonized, perishing and dying.
                    — Europe —
one image remains before you: faith and hope: a powerful
rugged man in cloth cap and blue shirt.
                    (When will you give him your love?)

O hungry, out-of-work, greedy, covetous, winners, losers,
breadless, moneyless, nude and dismembered.
                    — Europe —
one image remains before you: faith and hope: that stern
rugged man, a sickle in his hand.
                    (When will you give him your love?)

Behind the black smoke-stacks of the silent nocturnal factories
the silver sickle of the new moon is rising.

Call

Strike! Strike! Strike! —
the drums
the trumps
the bells
          — arouse!
Erupt in a whirl of excitement, elemental heart!
With frenzied hands hurl into hearts, into minds
firebrands of rapture
bombs of revolt
crimson cannon-balls of chaos
— mad moons and suns! —
Rise again illumined on the great day of man.
Lazarus, come forth!

Savonarola

High life of social good manners. *Beau monde* of sensational scandals. Booed retinue of a sacred order. Guards of legal plunder.

> Pure overpure
> smooth
> polished
> burnished
> white —
> white White Guards.

Priests of Mammon. Worshippers of Moloch. Pilgrims of a dead conscience. Heroes of venal embraces. Knights of manicure and pedicure. Champions of charity balls.

> Snob.
> Mob.
> Fop. Foppery.

Travelling salesmen in public security. Orators on supreme national interests. Heroes of the Constitution. Yellow press detectives. Robber barons of speculation. Fellow travellers of disaster. Argonauts of merchant banks. Apostles of the true will of the people.

> Life is a dream.
> Truth is in heaven alone.
> Earth is black.

Tricolour-sashed rhapsodists of a dead era. Conquistadors of civilization. Hussars of loot. Legal legates of peace.

> Pretorian guards of disgrace.

The Marseillaise

The end. The revolution crushed. The last fighters encircled in the last neighbourhood. Barricaded in the big building of the daily 'Red Flag'.

One large red flag, raised above the roof, is still waving and proudly smacking amidst the howl of the winter wind. The last flag. High above the last battle.

Meanwhile in the other parts of the town the old life was once more starting up with its regular colourful noise in the ancient streets, squares and market-places: buses, trams, horse-cabs, dealers forever in a hurry, stock-exchange jobbers forever in a sweat, perfumed ladies with pet dogs, servant-girls with baskets, nursemaids pushing prams, postmen loaded with letters.

The dreadful end was approaching. The final end. In the last neighbourhood.

The State Defence troops had surrounded the editorial offices of 'Red Flag' during the night. The shelling started at dawn. From the windows of the red building a few machine-guns sent their desperate rattle into nearby streets and courtyards.

Crack —

    sssssss —

          rrrrrr —

In ceaseless salvoes the mortars and mine-throwers of State Defence hurled heavy shells upon the building. Roof-tiles, bricks and concrete blocks crashed down noisily. The window-panes of neighbouring houses rattled in panic. The whole building of the daily 'Red Flag' split apart, convulsed by the ceaseless burst of shells. The machine-guns fell silent.

The smoke of the gun barrage mingled with the greenish vapour of poison gas, released like a thick cloud over the battered building. Now the remaining survivors would have to start jumping from the shattered windows of the upper floors and escape over the roofs of neighbouring buildings.

The revolution crushed. Complete quiet.

And at that moment of stifled silence came the soundof a hurdy-gurdy from some nearby park (with trained parrots and white mice, amidst a press of curious children) — the sounds of a hurdy-gurdy with the undaunted strains of the Marseillaise.

Bloodthirstily the machine-guns barked out after the last fighters of the revolution, now running over the roofs. In the other, now peaceful, parts of the town posters were being stuck up with the latest (savage yet reassuring) order of the Government, announcing the end of the revolution.

And the hurdy-gurdy, in impertinent ignorance, went on playing its usual piece — the Marseillaise.

The funeral

The victims of the revolution. Fourteen funeral carriages piled high with wreaths. Millions marching with red flags. Crowds on the pavements; indifferent faces, huddling into warm sable collars.

A respectable gentleman turns away in confusion. 'Hats off — there's a funeral passing', the rough voice of a worker tells him.

Other Titles from
FOREST BOOKS

Special Collection

THE NAKED MACHINE Selected poems of Matthías Johannessen.
Translated from the *Icelandic* by Marshall Brement. (Forest/
Almenna bokáfélagid)
0 948259 44 2 cloth £7.95   0 948259 43 4 paper £5.95   96 pages

ON THE CUTTING EDGE Selected poems of Justo Jorge Padrón.
Translated from the *Spanish* by Louis Bourne.
0 948259 42 6 paper £7.95   176 pages

ROOM WITHOUT WALLS Selected poems of Bo Carpelan.
Translated from the *Swedish* by Anne Born.
0 948259 08 6 paper £6.95   144 pages. Illustrated

CALL YOURSELF ALIVE? The love poems of Nina Cassian.
Translated from the *Romanian* by Andrea Deletant and
Brenda Walker. Introduction by Fleur Adcock.
0 948259 38 8 paper £5.95.   96 pages. Illustrated

RUNNING TO THE SHROUDS Six sea stories of
Konstantin Stanyukovich.
Translated from the *Russian* by Neil Parsons.
0 948259 04 3 paper £5.95   112 pages. Illustrated

East European Series

FOOTPRINTS OF THE WIND Selected poems of Mateya Matevski.
Translated from the *Macedonian* by Ewald Osers.
Introduction by Robin Skelton.
0 948259 41 8 paper £6.95   96 pages. Illustrated

ARIADNE'S THREAD An anthology of contemporary Polish
women poets. Translated from the *Polish* by Susan Bassnett and
Piotr Kuhiwczak. UNESCO collection of representative works.
0 948259 45 0 paper £6.95   96 pages.

POETS OF BULGARIA An anthology of contemporary
Bulgarian poets.
Edited by William Meredith. Introduction by Alan Brownjohn.
0 948259 39 6 paper £6.95   112 pages.

FIRES OF THE SUNFLOWER Selected poems by Ivan Davidkov.
Translated from the *Bulgarian* by Ewald Osers.
0 948 259 48 5 paper £6.95   96 pages. Illustrated

STOLEN FIRE Selected poems by Lyubomir Levchev.
Translated from the *Bulgarian* by Ewald Osers.
Introduction by John Balaban.
UNESCO collection of representative works.
0 948259 04 3 paper £5.95   112 pages. Illustrated

AN ANTHOLOGY OF CONTEMPORARY ROMANIAN POETRY
Translated by Andrea Deletant and Brenda Walker.
0 9509487 4 8 paper £5.00   112 pages.

GATES OF THE MOMENT Selected poems of Ion Stoica.
Translated from the *Romanian* by Brenda Walker and
Andrea Deletant. Dual text with cassette.
0 9509487 0 5 paper £5.00   126 pages   Cassette £3.50 plus VAT

SILENT VOICES An anthology of contemporary Romanian women
poets. Translated by Andrea Deletant and Brenda Walker.
0 948259 03 5 paper £6.95   172 pages.

EXILE ON A PEPPERCORN Selected poems of Mircea Dinescu.
Translated from the *Romanian* by Andrea Deletant and
Brenda Walker.
0 948259 00 0 paper £5.95.   96 pages. Illustrated.

LET'S TALK ABOUT THE WEATHER Selected poems of Marin Sorescu.
Translated from the *Romanian* by Andrea Deletant and
Brenda Walker.
0 9509487 8 0 paper £5.95   96 pages.

THE THIRST OF THE SALT MOUNTAIN Three plays by Marin Sorescu
(Jonah, The Verger, and the Matrix).
Translated from the *Romanian* by Andrea Deletant and
Brenda Walker.
0 9509487 5 6 paper £6.95   124 pages. Illustrated

VLAD DRACULA THE IMPALER A play by Marin Sorescu.
Translated from the *Romanian* by Dennis Deletant.
0 948259 07 8 paper £6.95   112 pages. Illustrated

Fun Series

JOUSTS OF APHRODITE Erotic poems collected from the Greek
Anthology Book V.
Translated from the *Greek* into modern English by Michael Kelly.
0 948259 05 1 cloth £6.95   0 94825 34 5 paper £4.95   96 pages